Journey
the Soul
of a Poet

Copy right © 2003 by Maya C. Houston
Journey The Soul of A Poet
ISBN 978-0-615-25176-9
Library of Congress Registration
TXu 1-093-858

Verses are taken from the Holy Bible, King James Version (NELSON 883CBG).

Published by:
Journee Publications
P.O. Box 901
Morrow, GA 30260
(404) 514-0733
journeepublications@yahoo.com
www.myspace.com/easypublishing

All rights reserved. No portion of this book may be reproduced in any form with out written permission of the publisher.

Cover designed by Maya C. Houston
Cover created by Marion Designs

Inside back cover photo: By Clyde Johnson
Krystal's Images
Charleston, SC 29407
krystalsimages@yahoo.com

To order additional copies, individual or wholesale please contact Journee Publications at the email address listed above or by calling (843) 345-5606 or (404) 514-0733

Printed in the United States of America.

Maya C. Houston

JOURNEY THE *Soul* OF A POET

A Poet's Journey Through Trials and Tribulations of Life

The Cover

The cover of my book is prophetic, God given. I really did not know what the cover should look like until I prayed about it. I racked my brain for weeks and I could not come up with a thing. I prayed and asked God to give me the cover. I put it aside and went on to put the book together. Within the next few days, this picture came to me. I saw the long road leading to the break of day with these beautiful mountains as a backdrop. I saw this dry land and a barren tree, which casts the shadow of a full tree. This is prophetic in so many ways and can be so for many people. The long road speaks to this journey we call life. The dry land represents the rough times in this life, the barren tree epitomizes the physical man and the way we see our selves and the way we feel most times when we are going through and trying to get to the promise of the mountaintop at dawn. The shadow of the full tree denotes that everything we need is already with-in. We must walk in the fullness of life, love, and in all that we hope to accomplish and become.

CONTENTS

About the author 7
Introduction 9
Acknowledgement 11
Work To Do 17
Geechee Girl 20
What I Love About Writing! 22
Gone Too Long 25
When We Use Too 28
Contagious 30
Only One In 33
Emotional Homicide 35
I Should've Had a V8 38
Crying 40
Are You Sure? 42
Get It Right 44
Actions Speak Louder Than Words 46
To Every king 49
Listen To My Heart 52
Positive Energy Always Creates Elevation 54
Just Thinking 56
Just Walk Away 59
No Weapons 62
Dragon Tails 65
Black Widow 71
Woman 74
Save Your Selves 77
Rain On Me 78
Priceless 80
Love 82

Seasons Change	85
Diamonds	87
Voyage	90
He Said	92
She Said	93
Be Mine	95
Smile	97
"Let Me Be Your Water"	99
Dream About Me	102
I'm Looking At You	104
Genesis	106
In The Beginning	109
King	112
Kryptonite	114
Can You Handle It?	116
I Want A Man	120
Never Had A Love	121
Put Together By God	123
I Want To Love You	127
Soul Mate	130
Husband	132
And So I Cry	134
We Raise Our Fists	137
Tell Your Children Stories	140
Wisdom's Pearls	143
Sugar Dish	144
God's Gifts To Me	147
The F.I.R.M.	149
Thank You!	151
Contact Page	152

ABOUT THE AUTHOR

MAYACeleste Houston entered the family circle of Truman, Mary, and Melody Houston on June 19, 1977. She was born at Medical University of South Carolina.

Maya was 36.5 weeks gestation, weighing 5lbs at birth she was placed in the intensive care unit for observation. After being in ICU for only a few hours, it was discovered that she had an intestinal problem called intersession. Intersession is a condition where the small intestine folds inwardly causing blockage, therefore any fluids taken in can't pass through the intestinal track which in turn causes vomiting with each feeding. After this condition was sited Maya was taken immediately to surgery. The procedure took approximately two hours. She was sent back to ICU for further observation and remained in ICU for approximately one week. Maya was sent home under the care of her mother and father and has since thrived very well. She attended New Israel Christian School from age 4 to 7. At 8 years of age she was enrolled at James Simmons Elementary School where she remained until she graduated to Rivers Middle School in 1989.

While still at Rivers Middle School in 1991 she became a junior varsity cheerleader for the Burke High School Bulldogs. She later made the bulldog's varsity team. However, after she graduated from Rivers Middle School in 1992 she attended Middleton High School for two years. Due to the lack of social organizations geared towards African American teenagers, Maya and a few of her newly found friends founded Omega Phi Nu. The first, and only sorority beginning with Omega. Omega Phi Nu began with approximately 20 girls, with Maya reigning as president. Although the faculty did not approve, Maya along with her friends fought to keep their club functioning. The club raised money by having bake sales, car washes, and other community events. In return theses girls went to the local orphanage, had cookouts and spent time with children less fortunate than themselves all in the name of Omega Phi Nu. Because of these pioneering teenagers other campus sororities came about. Omega Phi Nu remained in operation at the Middleton High School campus even years after Maya and her friends graduated. In her junior year she transferred to Burke High School. She attended vocational classes at Burke that year, then commuted to Garrett Academy of Technology where she obtain her cosmetologist's license in her senior year.

Maya graduated and received her High School Diploma from Burke High School in June of 1995. In 2002 she received a Network Administrator's Diploma from Beta Tech in Charleston, South Carolina. Maya now lives in Morrow Georgia with her daughter Zion where she works as a dental assistant and is presently attending Clayton State University.

INTRODUCTION

JOURNEY The Soul of a Poet is a candid view of my life and some of the people and situations I have encountered given to you in the form of poetry. Along the way I have learned some valuable lessons. I have formulated questions and I have found some answers. This book has allowed me to be open, honest, and reflective about my own growth. I pray that this journey will instill in women courage, wisdom, and self-love. I pray that our men will receive a message of tough love, direction, encouragement, and an understanding that we need them to take back their rightful positions in our lives (women & children) as husbands, fathers, brothers, and uncles.

We seem to have lost our way, forgotten our paths. My hope is to contribute to the reconstruction of the character of this generation. I have a craving to witness the meaningful core values we so prided our selves on some time ago. My focus is primarily on men and women as a combined whole. We as women must recognize our own worth and make it a point to recognize the worth of our men. Although men govern the vast majority of our civilization, we women shape the men.

Love your self then you can love others. Take this journey with me on my uphill fight to become confident, insightful, and comfortable about who I am as a woman. Prepare to read about my impulsive decisions and relationships, and notice me succumbing to my shallow desires then maturing and learning to master self, which is a continuous learning process.

Most every poem is introduced by a question or a moment of reflection and hindsight. I welcome you into my life and I pray that we can relate on one level or another. My desire is that as you read you will find yourself, begin to reflect, laugh, be encouraged, and grow with me! If only one word, one line, one poem, reaches one person, I will feel that my writing truly has purpose.

        Thank you for taking this journey with me.
        Peace and blessings.

ACKNOWLEDGEMENTS

THIS book is dear to me, but not nearly as dear as the people who inspired, encouraged, discouraged, hoped for, hope against, dreamed for and even damned my efforts. I thank each and every one of you. God is great and I need Him for all things! This accomplishment is proof of Romans 8:28-33 "All things work together for the good of them that love the Lord"
Romans 8:31, "If God be for us who can be against us?"
Romans 8:33, "I am God's elect!"
I thank Him for blessing me with the gift of expression. I take it seriously, and I see it as a ministry.

For those of you who are in the church and have been delivered from everything; praise God for that, I commend you. I ask that you not condemn me for where I am in my walk with Christ, just know that I am a work in progress. My hope is that you will see what you use to be, and celebrate! See yourself where you want to be, walk with me, heal with me, and grow with me. I hope to provoke conversations, change minds, give birth to new ideas, and change lives! If one word, one line, one poem touches one person then I will feel that my journey has tremendous purpose!

My mom and dad are two of my greatest supporters. Thank you Mom for coming out to the smoke filled clubs to hear me, you gave me courage. Daddy, thanks for not criticizing me, or judging me, you gave me the chance to choose wisdom, you gave me freedom and the ability to reach born knowledge.

To my pastor, Reverend Isaac J. Holt Jr., of Royal Baptist Church, located in North Charleston, SC, you believed in me when I was not sure of my self. You saw into me and took a chance by putting me before the congregation to speak when I didn't feel worthy. You gave me an enormous boost! You saw my work uncut, my most raw work and still you nurtured the God messages that were trying so hard to come through my carnal vernacular. You took a chance on me and advised me to go into print. For that I am graciously appreciative. I thank God for placing me in your flock.

Robert Ellington A.K.A. Poppa Robbie, one of my greatest teachers and a dear friend, I love you like a brother and I appreciate everything you have contributed over the years that have added to the birth of this book and to my way of free thinking. I am also grateful for the descriptive summary on the back of the book. I cannot imagine anyone else writing it, you are best qualified because you have witnessed and aided in my development over the years. Thank you!

Mr. Heyward of Ultra Beauty Hair Salon, you taught me to hold on to my dreams; that my dreams can and will come true. You said that I am not to let anyone tell me that I cannot do what my heart desires. You also told me, "Never let anyone tell you that you can not achieve your dreams. Be sure to follow your dreams!" For that, I am grateful.

My family is the absolute best! My aunts, uncles, and cousins all seem to believe I can do anything. They always showed me love and confidence by always creating a stage for me by asking and encouraging to me to write for different occasions. You guys will never know how much asking me to share at dinner and other gatherings helped me practice and refine my craft. All of you have built my confidence, and fed my desire.

I would not have moved forward with publishing as soon as I did if it had not been for two great men, Alfred Adams and Omar of Dewey Hill Publications. These two brothers took time from their busy schedules to sit with me, help me understand the industry and told me how to go about getting my message out. They shared certain knowledge and resources and I can't thank them enough!

I want to thank my ex-husband for failing to recognize my worth, and for not loving me right. Had it not been for his ill treatment I may not have tapped into my ability to declare the truth so ferociously in such a poetic way. Thanks!

Mrs. Lorinda D. Richards (Peachie) October 20, 1958 – March 27, 2006, an outstanding woman beautiful inside and out. Peachie put it to me plain, "This is really good, you need to do something with this, it would be a shame if you didn't. I am serious, promise me you will get them together, and publish them. I mean it." *So I did, I dedicate this moment to you. Love you, rest in peace.*

Finally, to my readers I am humbly grateful that you would even take the time to hear me. Words cannot express my gratitude!

For Zion, you inspire me....

To my matriarchs,
The late
Irene Houston & Virginia Taylor
two women of yesterday,
who made me the woman I am today.
Infinite love.

Tiffany R. Wright-Gregory,
Thanks for always believing in me.
You said this day would come!
Love you.

Dorothea L. T. Gadsden (Cotton)
Thank you for always being there for me,
you are one in a million, more like a sister.
Whenever I call, you never ask why
you only ask where and when.
I thank God for you.

Shawnikia Lawson-Patterson
&
Shawndora Seabrook (Shawnie)
These women have such style and grace.
Thanks for keeping me dressed tastefully
for photo shoots and appearances.

This is my life, come journey with me, I got work to do!

WORK TO DO

If Truman aint my daddy then my mother has got be the original Mary and me the baby Jesus! Cause he's the only man that stood proud and said he was blessed on the day I was born. Since the day I entered this world satan and his helpers been out to get me, a gifted little girl! From causing me to choke from within till I turned blue but God sent me back with vengeance, said you got work to do!

Just a few years after that one close to me took the most from me he acted out his adult type fantasies on little girls in the family including me. In a short time I came to find this boy brandish his gun at me, he didn't know this was fun to me! To his surprise, I was ready to die and had already contemplated suicide so I looked him square in the eyes and said if you pull it you better use it! I need a sound track for my life and I want Most Def and Common to write the music.

Just a few weeks later another was a bit bolder, he put the gun to my head cocked the hammer and was hold'n. I smacked his hand, moved to the side, talked a little garbage then repeated. In my bravado I succeeded, sad to say a few weeks later he was shot multiple times, paralyzed from the waist down, I frown and in my spirit I hear it; touch not my anointed do my prophet no harm. In an arms length of time I found myself staring down the barrel of a gun for the third time.

He said, "you gone go home, get your clothes and you come'n with me" all I could think of was my family, my mom what would they tell her? I still don't know how I got out, the rest of the night is a blur.

Fast-forward to 2005 my first-born came my third child, but the only one alive and her father long gone. Known him half my life never thought twice that he would be absentee.

FAT-HER he did me, FATHER her he did she and now we need a daddy. A real man, one that can make decisions based on the needs of others outside of self. One who knows that any germ can be a donor.

Father present at the time of conception, concept of daddy a deception, it is a blessing to create new life. My past told me I wasn't good enough life just a little rough but I'm gone get it right. While I may not be the Messiah these messages shut up in me like fire, yeah you can call me Jeremiah and after all I've been through there's more to come, still I got work to do...

Charleston, one of the oldest slave states filled with rich, deep rooted African culture and beautiful people. The people here have several different dialects all falling under one name geechee from the language Gullah. Key components of Gullah people are rice, sweat grass basket weaving, storytelling, preservation of culture and strength....

GEECHEE GIRL

I'm a southern girl born in the palmetto
& crescent moon state. Some say I'm
prissy and others say
I'm hood. To be constantly
misunderstood is that
my fate?

I'm a Carolina sweetie, foreigners call
me geechee, I get a little
rowdy at times but really I'm the creator
of the peace treaty!
Meaty, thick, yeah that's from dem rice
and grits and I'm proud of da
mixed languages that come these lips!
Gullah: is a combination of many different
African languages and English.

Perceived to be ignorant, conceived from
the need of self preservation
dem white boys was putt'n my four
mothers and fathers through
mental, emotional and sleep depravation.
(Devastation on dem plantations!!!)
So the implication that geechee
is a joke, if chewed on properly
will make you choke!

See, through it all we overcame, and is
known in the U.S. is known as
one of the oldest living cultures in
this game. Oh, and I got news for ya
wikipedia lists Gullah as people that
live in the low-country of
South Carolina, Florida and Georgia.
We created new languages, and new
ways of life. The resilience came
from brilliance, always able to
bounce back!

So all you sons and daughters from near
dem waters, don't be shame to
claim the geechee name cause them bouy
ain know wha on ya brain!

WHAT I LOVE ABOUT WRITING!

That's what I love about writing!
Most things come and go,
sometimes it's hard to go with the flow.
They say all good
things come to an end but not this love
affair I have with my pen, or
should I say my ink? Just think one pen
through get another, red, green,
black, or blue what ever suits you.
Go with the rhythm of your pen it
points out hot lyrics
again and again.

That's what I love about writing,
at the tip of your fingers
like lightening
as quickly as you think it your pen is
writing. Writing never fails you,
in fact it heals what ever ails you! It's
comforting and therapeutic. I love
writing like my dad loves his old Buick!
I am writing and talking to you as I
read back I end up
talking to me too.

Man this is cool I wish they had me
writing more when I was in school
writing allows me to put myself on
paper and invite you to behold all the
words imprinted on my soul. Come with
me and bring a pen, let's trade
gifts! I love writing with friends.

JOURNEY THE SOUL OF A POET

Most times we let our physical desires cloud our better judgment and the people that have not been gone nearly long enough, we feel that they've been gone too long....

GONE TOO LONG

You've been gone from me too long,
I can tell because the symptoms are too strong.
I can't even sleep.
Your sweet love to me is like focus factor,
I need it to...I need it to... um... what was I saying?
Oh yeah
as a matter of fact your sweet love puts me exactly
where I need to be. Focus factor yeah that's you for me.
I think I finally found my connect physical, mental, and
emotionally. As we conjure spirits, moans and groans
make love's lyrics.
The sweet love that you give to me cracks my back,
keeps me on track; damn boo where you at?
You've been gone from me too long, come back home
baby. I think I'm gonna need some help!
I now understand what Luther was saying, because

"I'd rather have bad times with you, than good times
with someone else, I'd rather be out in a storm,"
cause baby you are my safe and warm.
Damn, how you all in my dome?
You've been gone from me too long baby
come back home.

JOURNEY THE SOUL OF A POET

This is for the grown and sexy baby..............

Can you imagine what it might've been like to witness the creation of the universe? I mean to see stars and planets take shape, to watch the rings form around Saturn. To taste orange before it was a color, to be the glide of an eagle on high, ooooohwe!

WHEN WE USE TO....

When we use to make love I saw Mars,
Saturn and Venus take shape.
I mean you made me taste the colors orange,
violet, and blue.
You were inside me and sometimes
I felt like I was inside of you.

As we levitated still intertwined my mind
projected planets spinning out of control,
we were in the center creating a whole new realm.
When we use to make love I saw the sky's orange-
reddish hue, I saw an eagle glide and sore upon wings
with the grace that only God can issue.

When we use to make love I would mirror you.
In your eyes I saw me. It's no wonder God blessed us
with "A Beautiful Journee."
When we use to make love,
I saw the planets being formed,
I tasted colors orange, violet, and blue.
I felt celestial beings spinning into another time and
space and taste was magnified.
Your lips were sweet and tender
like firm ripened peaches.
Your bodies sweat just as sweet.
I miss your man nectar

When we use to make love, I don't know about
you but for me it was spiritual.

No picture can depict, no lyrical free verse
can be spit to reveal the for real
understanding that we share much deeper than
care, the highest elevation of love....
when we use to.

CONTAGIOUS

Yellow sheets against my barely covered brown body,
candle light flickering Kahlua on ice. Right about now
I'm feeling kind of nice.
Brown velvet skin on display, as I
spread pink sunshine shows
you a brand new day.

**"You're contagious, touch me baby
and give me what you got"**

Sip from my cool drip to slow down your hot...

"Sexy baby drive me crazy, drive me wild"

This session's so tight you don't know if
you should cry or smile.
Yeah you right that kinky stuff's my style.
I'll take my clothes
off and leave my boots on. Even when
you're not here I feel you
all in my bones, it's not only a physical
but a mental "jones".

We stimulate one another's erogenous zones,
you squeeze me
I groan you make me want to moan.
Even in the presence of others

when you're not here I feel so alone.

"You're Contagious, touch me baby
give me what you got
Sexy baby drive me crazy, drive me wild....."

JOURNEY THE SOUL OF A POET

No matter how hard you love someone
who is not in love with you, you'll be the only one in

ONLY ONE IN

When you walk away the way you do
I don't think you understand
the emotional throws you put me through.
Don't get it twisted and
think I expect this marriage to supply
an all easy all smooth life.
I know there will be rain and strain and
through it all I will remain
your loving wife.

For better or worse, for richer or poor,
till death do us part. But to be
pushed aside and see you walk away always takes
a toll on my heart.
Communication and understanding are
only two key necessities to
our marriages' survival. Miscommunication
or a lack there of causes
misunderstandings.

Four months and
counting and comparing the time
we've been and the time we're suppose to be
makes our four months
seem like only four hours to me.

Marriage is not to be taken or entered into lightly nor should it end prematurely, however some marriages should not take place at all. Till death do us part is the sacred vow. So what if the death is a spiritual one or an emotional one should we part?

EMOTIONAL HOMICIDE

How can you be mad at me for trying to escape this emotional rape? Why should I stand by and allow you to take all I've got? It is so sad to see how my other half would bludgeon me mentally. The wife of a man who loved me not.

We were supposed to be one you and me whole, unfortunately I ended up fighting a battle to salvage my soul. You were killing me from with in.
Had it made the papers head lines would have read;

"Emotional homicide, when should a married man put away his pride?"

Each night in my mind I scrub with reasoning the bruises and blemishes left behind on my soul. How could you have been so unkind, then pretend to be blind to the fact that mentally and emotionally, you broke my back!

Love and partnership this marriage did lack.
You didn't have the "sack" to come correct and treat your wife with respect after your wrongs were counted. Didn't you think malice was mounting?

The stakes are too great now, I've lost too
much of me now and earlier on I vowed never to
let it be like this.

You walk around appearing to be remised, while
"sitting high" and "looking low" that cave man
mentality has got to go!

See you'll never deserve that special lady just as you
never deserved me. I had to learn self love in
order to be free.

No longer the emotionally battered, neglected at
times disrespected helpmate.

I am the survivor, strong and beautiful, higher in
Christ, wiser in life. The one you tried to negate
mentally. I was your wife, supposedly for life your
mate, and I decided to escape that mental and
emotional rape.

JOURNEY THE SOUL OF A POET

To all the ladies with the God given gift to conceive life, to nurture it in your womb, and to bring it forth through the birth canal. Do not take that ability lightly. It is a great responsibility and no man should tell any woman, what ever her choice is, what she needs to do with her body and the life that she is bonding with. A bond that begins with fatigue, morning sickness, headaches, light headedness and countless other ailments.

However, we as women, sacred enough to give birth, mold and shape these lives, must be more responsible. We must be selective about the man we allow into our hollowed places. As men sacred enough to be a major component in this spiritual event, you must do the same.

As co-creators of life we must make better choices and stand by them. Men should be husbands and fathers. Women should require respect and position before we "assume the position."

I SHOULD'VE HAD A V8

You weren't scared to f*#@ or scared to
bust now you want
me to get rid of what's part of us.
Everything I needed you for has already taken Place.
Maybe you were just here to plant the seed so
I could give birth to God's grace.

Stress me, neva that this type of thing is common place.
So lift up yo skirt, go on hit da dirt, do work
cause this lil one's life already has worth.

You were here today and gone tomorrow but
I'm gone raise this princess not to focus on that sorrow.
Hollow a#$ promises bout a bond we
had since we was kids.
A whole lot a good dat did. Messed around now my
period's late, and where you at with yours.
I shoulda had a V8.

Cry until you know you are whole all by yourself. Cry, reflect, take self-inventory, and embrace who you are and begin to move toward who you want to be. Crying is the beginning stage of the soul's healing process...

CRYING

Crying on the inside
but the tears won't come outside.
Lord please lead me,
but don't let this bleed me emotionally.
All the sins I have thought about committing
would delete me.
I thought I had found the man that would complete me.
Not realizing I was already completed.
I just hope your blessings and forgiveness is not depleted.

Don't ask me if you don't want to know and do not take me if you are not ready to go! Be sure that this is what you want.

ARE YOU SURE?

Now you sure this is what you want?
Don't ask for it cause you just might get it.
My love ain't no joke, so don't laugh
and don't let it be no game I ain't the same as your
average. I am that lady about whom most
brothers be thinking love, marriage then a
baby carriage.

Don't disparage the fact that I can decipher
a mack a mile away. Once you enter it's
hard to get out, make sure your heart precedes
what flows from your mouth. I doubt that
you even know what you are getting
yourself into.

Cherry flavored lips and seductive hips
on an ebony angel with eyes that tell
about thighs from whence you came,
it's a damn shame how some brothers
play love's games.

See some brothers got it twisted, we can be their mistresses. We can be the ladies that have their babies and maybe even take care of the babies they had before we met. But what they don't get is that we truly love. We want that same dedication, that same love and that same loyalty but too often some how they miss the mark or just don't try these brothers need to get it right!

GET IT RIGHT

See I'll massage ya heart like Neil did Trinity in the Matrix and bring you back to life, ride or die, not a side chick see I'm a wife, #1 pick.

Love ya like when grandparents had names like Johnny and Virginia. I 'm talk 'n dat real sh** not dat make believe pretend sh** in da morning cooking eggs and grits, hand you yo lunch pale just before I give you a kiss.

No wolf man, no jodies, aint try'n to shoot a blitz. Know and understand I'm more than just ass and tits. Think before you speak, look at you and see me, because the same thighs that give you pleasure gave you life. Nine months was measured and you could call me b*tch before you utter wife?!?

Get It Right

Synchronize your conscious with your conduct...

ACTIONS SPEAK LOUDER THAN WORDS

On this journey together, started out
one you and one me as we are joined
there's just "one we." No turning back, no shows
or acts.
You are here with me, then be here for me, ONLY me.
I would never ask for what I would
not give, our life together we should both
live faithfully, truthfully, lovingly,
and in a manner pleasing to God. So do not
take me if you are not ready to go.

This is a once in a lifetime experience to be
carried out, respected and cherished till death.
These words are from my heart not just talk,
so if you can't get with what's
written then you might as well walk!

No chicks on the side, no mistresses
outside the bride, just me.
It aint no fair if I got to share. I mean
I don't want you if you can't deal
with the fact that you can no longer mack
Action speaks louder than words
so say what you want cause I'm not hearing
what you say, I'll see what you do.

The words from your lips drip, drip,
drip then action in your ways say the opposite.
Just do right, keep it real I'd hate to
leave but I will. It can be two days, two hours,
before or ten days, ten hours, two
years after, it'd be a disaster but
I would have to be out!

JOURNEY THE SOUL OF A POET

Marriage is a partnership. Husband the head and the wife the helpmate. Not the tail, not the servant girl, but more like the neck! We all know that the head cannot move without the neck! They work together, one is useless without the other. Neither more important, both absolutely necessary.

TO EVERY KING

So you say your happiness is my duty.
My J-O-B is to be bare-footed,
pregnant and in the kitchen.
What are you sniff'n? Negro please
slowly fall down to your knees.
Bare assed and toothless, dick in hand
and my cum in your mouth. You are not the
only royal one in this house!
King can't be king with out his queen
you'd only be a prince know
what I mean?

Stop acting like a stone aged boy, grow into
your crown, come down
and sit level with your opposite equal.
King being the head, bread winner,
nurturer, and the center of the family unit.
Queen being the neck, nurturer, bread winner
and the center of the family unit.

Same thing, same thing, different order.
Family needs me, family
needs you, same thing same thing
different order. I need you, you need me
same thing, same thing different order.
Order, order, order, bring some order

to this chaotic way of being. Open our
mind's eye I am so tired of us not
seeing we are responsible for our own
contentment. Make a commitment
to love you then you can love me.

The neck is to be protected and respected,
the head is to respected and
protected as the two are connected let
us connect spiritually, mentally,
emotionally, and while physically connecting
you to me. How could you not
see you in me?

JOURNEY THE SOUL OF A POET

The More you cry and evaluate yourself, you will learn who you are and you will begin to listen to your heart more. Then you will recognize when others are willing to listen too.

LISTEN TO MY HEART

Rest your head on my breast and
read the beats of my heart.
Now do all that it asks
I hope its happiness will last.
Love me down and make me feel fine.

You know what I want?
I want you to make love to my mind.
Be my man and please be my friend, I really
don't want to have to start all over again.
I just want you to love me and keep it real.
Good or bad you can always tell me how you
feel. Friends for life, lovers for even longer,
let's take our time build this thing
brick by brick that will make
it stronger.

As you begin to listen to your self you will learn that it is absolutely imperative that you are careful who and what nourishes your soul, and who you allow to be in your cipher. Your spirit swallows up everything in the atmosphere, regurgitates it later in some way, shape or form, regurgitation usually happens when you least expect it, and oddly you may not even notice it. Therefore, you must to be mindful of what you take in because it will definitely come back out

POSITIVE ENERGY ALWAYS CREATES ELEVATION

Be sure to choose what energies
you will allow to influence your state
of being by carefully selecting who and
what will be in your cipher, who and
what will feed you and who and
what you will receive into your spirit,
because your spirit
leads your life.
PEACE

Why wait to be told what part we hold in the lives of those we first choose. Sometimes you got to know when to fold...

JUST THINKING

I've been trying to control my urges and slow down
my thoughts of you. I've been fighting my feelings
and trying to limit my dealings but still I end up eating,
breathing, sleeping and craving fantasies of you too.

You can't be at all good for me, because badly all I want
is you. In this written confession, my
hidden verbal expressions I bare.
Wouldn't dare speak seriously about how
dear you are to me.
I can't begin to count the endless praises
my soul leaks
for this man who seeks only to be
my boy toy.

And though I understand that at the
hands of another fem
you require refuge from this reality.
The reality that people and seasons
do change while some
of our needs may stay the same.
The same reality that won't
allow you to give me a fair 100% is
causing me to pull away from
you and block out any possibility of
being consciously intimate with

you on any level other than surface
pretend verses over the phone.

Before I give myself to this perilous game,
before I fall victim to your reckless aim,
before I end up just another f@%ked dame
I'll re-nig and we can just call it.
Game.

As you live, you learn about your self. What you want, what you don't want, what you deserve, what to accept and what to walk away from. Surely there will come some times when you will have to just walk away.

JUST WALK AWAY

I decided to walk away from them both,
like a bad plane crash leaving me
with only minor bruises and scratch.

As I emerged from the smoke film cloud
of deceit, I gave all I had and in return I got an
empty receipt.

Sounds like defeat? No not to me because when
you leave it in the Master's hands He'll bring your
enemies to your feet.

JOURNEY THE SOUL OF A POET

Luke 20:42-43

And David himself said in the book of Psalms,
the Lord said unto my Lord, sit thou on my right hand,
Till I make your enemies your footstool.

Remember as you go through, and
times seem so hard you can't see
your way, it is always darkest just
before the day! So hold on and
know that no weapons formed
against you shall prosper!
Isaiah 54:17

NO WEAPONS

Married, divorced, and two buried babies.
Maybe, I should give up now.
I've been mistreated, lied to, lied on,
talked about and mislead.
What now? Give victory to the devil and
live life as the dead?
My nearest and dearest are slaves to drugs
most that approach me aren't
men just thugs.

I've gone to the house where heads smoke crack
to pull my Kings out so they can try to bounce back.
But my back ends up against the wall and in the spiritual
I watch a people rise, while in the
physical they appear to fall.
All these weapons formed against me have failed.
Like the postal services come rain, sleet, snow or hail,
I'll give praises to the great creator, bless the natural born
haters, look back over my life and
still let the praises flow!
No!! No weapons formed against
me shall prosper!

JOURNEY THE SOUL OF A POET

Isaiah 54:17
"No weapon that is formed against thee
shall prosper; and every tongue
that shall rise against thee in judgment
thou shall condemn. This is the heritage
of the servants of the Lord and their
righteousness is me, saith the Lord."

Know that obstacles will come, weapons
will be formed but they cannot prevail
according to the word of the Lord.
So don't be discouraged, do not back down
and do not turn around call them out!
Tell your obstacles what thus says the Lord.
Know that the threats are empty,
and the weapons are not loaded
they cannot prosper...

Often times most people don't know what they want, and when they discover what it is that they do want they're too afraid to receive it. They end up running from what they are yearning for most and fighting what they naturally adhere to. It is a bottomless pit that leaves us chasing tail.

DRAGON TAILS

He is not ready for me. It's like run'n upon
a dragon shaded by "darkness," only a
portion of its tail at light.

He grabs hold thinking that small portion
of tail is all there is until the dragon swings
around full thrust, throwing its explorer for a loop.

Putting him face to face with truth. His hands open,
lifting from the "tail" but now he's hooked at the wrists
being thrown by these mental and emotional lifts. He
learns that what he thought was
just "tail" has heart, mind and soul.
Turns out to be whole, total and complete.
His mental and emotional thermometers overheat!

He is not ready for me. He won't conceive of me, but
he'll be intrigued by me, want to hold on to me and my
understanding which has a circumference of 360 degrees
that will eventually sway him and he too will fall into
this bottomless pit of yearning for, yet running from, of
clinging yet repelling.

I am 360 degrees around and 33 degrees
deep, most brothers
can't fathom my brain waves even when I am asleep!

My mental quake will shake any flake
that aint got his affairs
in order. Come seek the daughter of Isis, this Queen be
the nicest!

Put out your joints, forget your spliffs and meditate this,
most brothers think I'm a myth! Just because I
"overstand" my man and how to treat him who-
ever he be, how-ever he be.

Truth is I've learned through him to see me.

The healing Process: Learning to love yourself

There is a time to hurt and a time to heal, and most of us want to heal without going through the actual process. Not going to happen! Think of it, you fall, you get a bruise and it looks pretty bad. As the skin begins to grow over the wound there is a scab that is formed and the pain is still there but the skin is actually getting better. It looks worse and sometimes it seems to hurt more, but in time that sore is gone. Sometimes there's a scar that's left behind and other times there's not. The goal is to turn our scars into tools, to learn from them, gain strength and knowledge of self and continue to press on. Eventually the skin will look as good as new....

You feel that love has failed you so you block out every possible chance for its true beauty and you begin to hurt others. The problem with that is as a woman, nurturer, co-creator and giver of life. Your actions and mentality contradict everything you were created for. You were created to love. To give love and receive love we need love. What great creators have you known to destroy without the purpose of building again?

Destroy only to build again.

Jeremiah 1:10

See, I have this day set thee over the nations and the
kingdoms, to root out and to pull
down and to destroy and
to throw down, to build and to plant.

BLACK WIDOW

My friends call me the "Black Widow"
in that I sweetly, slowly
subjugate my men mentally. Then later deliver a physical
challenge. The challenge so blissful, so sensual the human
male senses never register quite the same anymore. I can
tame any whore.

All it took was one dose and their hooked! Then they'd
have the nerve to get scared and prepare
themselves for the worst
after I've given them my best.
From the start I opened my heart
and when it was too good to be true, what is it do you
think they try to go and do?

They put their lives on the shelf start scheming and just
play themselves. Now they can't sleep,
don't want to eat. Can't even
concentrate as they try to contemplate how they're going
to compete with my strong mind and sweet tasting
behind.
I tell them, "to the back of the line!"

Acting as if they didn't know this world is mine. You
should've taken it while I was giving it. A sister giving
you a love life and you just killing it. Sad,
sad thing, you gone learn about

me cause see pimpin aint easy. You've
got to get to know me
in order to "know" me and even then you won't understand me.

The man and the woman the creator helped
to create me don't
even understand this mystery! I'm a puzzle, a muzzle on
the mind of the greatest genius personality.
some call me "Black Widow" while others yell out
"Abstract," I've got some
mental manifestations that will blow out your back...

As you mature and you begin to embrace life, you realize that you are not a Black widow you are woman instead. You stop wanting to kill and destroy you begin to have a craving, a deep desire to build and encourage.

JOURNEY THE SOUL OF A POET

WOMAN

I'm da mad trash talka, dat do da dang thing walka,
wisdom comes to me when it's time to get wise just
like reefer smoke on me when herb wanna get high!

I'm da Mary that had da Baby Jesus,
I'm da name you call on every time
somebody sneezes.

I'm da mystery that built the sphinx,
I'm what they look'n fo when they talk'n
bout them miss'n links!

I'm da one fem. that make most brothas stop and think!
I'm dat "M-Fa" that Absolute drinks!
I'm your companion, your friend;
I'm the beginning and the end.

I am woman

What ever happened to the kind of women that carried themselves in a manner to be respected? Sitting with their feet crossed at the ankles, requiring a chase, nurturing children, encouraging men, building moral fiber by passing on much needed wisdom? Where are the men? The men that worked hard, and provided for their families. The men that courted the woman, loved and raised little boys and girls to be productive men and women? What has happened? Titus 2

Titus 2

"But as for you speak the things that are proper for sound doctrine: that the older men be sober, reverent, temperate sound in faith, in love, in patience.
The older women likewise, that they be reverent in behavior, not slanderers, not given to much wine, teachers of good things.
That they admonish the young women to love their own husbands, to love their children, to be discrete, chaste, good, respectful to their own husbands
that the word of God may not be blasphemed."

SAVE YOUR SELVES

Black men unite treat every sister as
she is your guiding light.
Black women stand tall, hold your heads up. Hookers,
hoochies and hoes, I am fed up!
Don't get me wrong dress as you please.
I have grown to appreciate our many
styles and diversities
But I don't understand why sisters
have to skeeze. You are so
valuable more precious than your weight in gold. This
self-destructive behavior is not worth
the decay of your soul.

RAIN ON ME

Another lonely night waiting on you, knowing
this isn't right. With in I am hosting a fight and I
imagine to your delight my tears don't matter,
my emotions they scatter. I want to hold on to you
but you leave me nothing to hold on to.

I mean, what's a girl to do? I want to say that my heart
can't take no more but that's not true. I fear I will always
love you. I only wish you loved me back
enough to stop putting
me through the things you put me through.

You ask me to be understanding and now I feel like I am
standing under all that is important to you and the hand
I am playing is bound to lose. Makes me
think I expect too
much from you. When all I need is for
you to say what you
mean, mean what you say and call if you got delayed
because here I'm thinking you're on your way!

I've got so much more that I want to say
but I don't want to do it this way and you are not giving
me the time of day.
Why do I keep trying? You build me up to let me down
now I'm like Ashanti walking around all "foolish"
asking God to "rain on me and take this pain from me."

Valentine's Day card..$4.00
Candy...$7.99
Collect calls from juvenile detention center..........$2.99/min
Being there for a friend...Priceless!
Birthday gift $289.00
Birthday cake $7.99
Born Knowledge .... Priceless!
Box of envelopes..$1.99
Book of stamps..$7.99
Pack of ink pens $2.99
Letters of encouragement to the local jail .... Priceless!

PRICELESS

Childhood letters to juvie-hall, my dad was
mad as hell about those collect calls.
You were my first, first love and the man
I learned to be king.
It was like knowing you was my first
knowledge of a pharaoh.

I knew of kingdoms where Queens were
held high and Black men were of high
esteem too. As I got to know you despite
what you did I got to see this history
true in you. I knew everything I didn't know
I knew. Then you named me,
helped me become me and know who
I am. I mean my feelings of pride,
self love and the need to be f-r-e-e totally
now has a name.

"Queen Solar"

King, thank you for being who you are. Who knew we
were building me from with in?
The things you taught me while I was trying to teach you
still blows my mind today.
K-I-N-G in your own right. You know what I need from
you still? Is for you to fight.
Fight to stay on top,

Fight to stay off the block,
Fight to recognize your own self worth and live.
Live what you are worth here on this earth. Priceless!

You are priceless!

Queen Solar Magnificent

Love is such a heavy word, often taken and spoken way too lightly. In-fact most people using the word don't fully understand its meaning, its multitude or its power. I use to think that the only constant in life was change, as I live I am learning that another constant is love if it is real. Love holds on, love is ever strong, love forgives, love endures, and it never fades. With time it only grows. Love is infinite, love is...

LOVE

Love makes a way and that way is made forever,
never forgotten never lost. True love has no limits,
no specific price or cost. Money may pave a way but
over time the dollar amount will be misconstrued the
reason
will be mixed in with other debts that were paid and
money
stuffed cards for the holidays will fade away, but not love.

Time and deeds may fade away but not love.
Love makes a way that extends over continents, keeps
up with leaps and bounds yet still shows up when
one is down love will make a way!
Love does not come with conditions, it does not change
with the weather or the "weather" nots.
Loves is, and love makes a way.

Love is patient and love is kind. Love is listening,
learning,
knowing, growing, love is showing new concepts, sharing
beautiful thoughts. Love is beauty that happens deep
in the mind. **Love loves** no matter what love will
make a way. Love stands strong always no matter what
love stands. Not distance nor depth nor height, nor
principalities can come between love because love is and
love will find a way.

JOURNEY THE SOUL OF A POET

I Corinthians 13:4-5, 7-8

"Charity (love) suffers long, and is kind;
Charity envies not; charity vaunted not itself, is not
puffed up, does not behave itself unseemly,
seeks not her own is
not easily provoked, thinks no evil.
Bears all things, believes all things, hopes all things
endures all things.
Charity never fails."

It is so hard to know if you have found a lasting relationship. In this day and age love relationships don't seem to mean as much nor do they last very long. You really have to fight together in order to weather the storms of life and remain in sync. If it's what you want all you can do is hope and pray that you'll grow together

SEASONS CHANGE

I don't know if I told you, my every dream is to hold you. All that I learn new and old, all that I will experience and go through I hope to share with you. When life presents some sort of physical or emotional harm of any kind, comfort's arms are yours in my mind. As seasons change and winters become spring again, I hope we will stay the same.

Black men: One of God's most beautiful creations. Strong, with the ability to be gentle and responsive with chances of being uncaring.
Black women: A phenomenal formation by God and the other part of man's beauty. Woman formidable enough to be tender and most times compassionate with the propensity to be callous. Together the two are an impressive pair when all the rules are thrown out, pride is pushed aside and the two are lead by their soul's own true yearnings, you get diamonds! For all the brothers who are underappreciated and misunderstood, sitting blind in these diamond mines just waiting on time. Life is a process and the choices you make can be intense heat. "In order for a diamond to form, the earth must heat up to 2200 degrees Fahrenheit. Extreme heat, combined with pressure, and a long period of time produces a rare and precious commodity."
Black men....

DIAMONDS

My diamond in the rough, but no that's not enough.
My rose that sprung from concrete so street
but still so gentle, so sweet.

My Osyrus, others come beside us cause we the nicest.
I am his other side, his Isis! We are one like
Father, Son and
Holy Spirit or Osyrus, Isis and Horace.
You infidels bore us, abhor us,
when really you should adore us!

Must be the mis-education of a
nation on the essence of relations. So sit
back and hear as I ejaculate
into your ears for life these jewels of love.

Forget everything you know, relax and let go as I
emancipate your soul,
bring you back 360 and make you whole.

Often People will be drawn to you because of the God message inside you. We all have God guided revelation and purpose to be passed on to people we meet from time to time. Not everyone is to be an intimate partner some meetings are just to exchange important information and experiences so that one or both parties can get to the next level in this journey called life.

It is a beautiful thing to share the most
simple pleasures and treasures of life with
someone who values you the same as you value
them. Our greatest voyage is true love...

VOYAGE

I want to voyage to Mali, Guinea, and the
Ivory Coast with you.
I want to walk through the hoods of
Africa and greet current connections
to our ancestors with you too.

I want to go through and choose names
for our children with help from
the elders of the Malinke village.
I want to hum ritual chants as you sing
and romance the djembe drum. Oh yeah yeah.

I want to await your face close to mine
under the African Sky.
Soaking wet, I welcome your silhouette as
behind you the sun sets.
In our hut only a few intimate pieces
invoking spiritual energies
which connect you to me, me to you, us to the hut and
the hut to the universe.

Loving you is so easy there's no need to rehearse....

I want to voyage. I want to voyage to Angola,
Mozambique and
Botswana with you. I'd swim the
Nile just to kiss the smile of you.

Wrestle crocodiles for you too, one me and one you are
my favorite two.

I want to voyage, can we voyage?
I want to voyage with you.

HE SAID...

Warm vanilla chocolate
pillows N sheets, something to
warm the feet. Remembered
words suit me to be happy and at peace.
This dream my Lord has saved me.
To dream I have my pillows N sheets.
(Akil Pritchard)

SHE SAID...

Strawberries and Cream
what becomes a man with no
dreams? Emptiness and despair,
who more than I could care?
Pillows and sheets may warm
your feet but I pray that there are
words I could say that may warm
your heart. Getting back to your
start; warm vanilla chocolate and
strawberries and cream, tell me
what says your dreams?

Simply put, let's stay together.

BE MINE

Sun lights up blue skies
I see forever in your eyes.
Warm colors, be mine.

The first time I saw a full moon in the middle of the day I was amazed at it's beauty, moved by God's power and ability to do all things as He sees fit and I was grateful. That moment taught me to expect the unexpected and that the best is yet to come! It made me smile. Just as in true love, it comes when you least expect it and it's beauty is amazing.

SMILE

Each moment that I spend with you is like the first time I saw the day sky's moon as full and beguiling as the hazel in your eyes.
Smile...

The way you make me smile. Just to see your face, taste your sweet lips and feel your finger tips on my hips brings a smile. You have a unique style that drives me wild, a sweet personality, a man of principles, and old fashioned values. Who wouldn't want to have you!?
Smile...

Smile for me the way you make me smile by just entering a room, smile. Smile for me the way you make me smile by whispering sweet nothings into my ear, I love to hear you say "what's up baby? I got you."
Cause you damn sure do. Smile...

Smile to the rhythm of my heart, smile from beginning to end and from end to start. Just smile upon me with your peace, your wisdom, and your love. You are truly a blessing and must have been sent from above.

Water, strong, fluid, nourishing and causes life to grow. The correct flow of water can put out fires or generate electricity. I can recall the elders saying, "a steady drip of water can wear a hole in a rock so be patient, never give up, and be strong like water baby."

LET ME BE YOUR WATER

Allow me to pour myself upon you and all your dreams. Let me nurture what is already there although to others it may not seem. Will you let me be your water? See most folks don't want to water what's "not there" they don't care until they see in the physical your ability to produce.

But I want to give you a boost. I wasn't there in the beginning but maybe I can water your roots. From a small bud to a huge oak tree I hope you will self evaluate, then "me" evaluate, then "we" evaluate and as you re-evaluate the three you'll come to know the truth in my sincerity. Take a sip. Just let me spray you with commitment. Can I spray with a love of uncondition? Be submerged by me, as I can be a pool of ever-flowing tenderness and devotion only if you'll let me. See <u>sometimes</u> you seem to be water proof and I don't know why when all I want to do is shower you with high-esteem, honor you and flood you with compassion.

Why won't you drink of me? I don't mean, "taste" as you do time and again, I mean imbibe. Am I acceptable to "taste" but not good enough to swallow?
Absorb me, soak me up and realize that your vision is my own. I'm in this thing with you but sometimes, somehow I feel like I am so alone.

Take me in and know what I am worth, for your value to

me goes far beyond the "rocks and dirt" you are budding from. Come, it can be done slowly. Sip of me, let me be your water. Allow me to pour myself upon you and all your dreams and watch us grow.

Our dreams can all become a reality
if we let them....

JOURNEY THE SOUL OF A POET

DREAM ABOUT ME

Dream of me loving you for rest of my life.
Dream about me kissing you with tears in
my eyes as you ask me to be your wife!

Dream of me fulfilling your every fantasy. Just
dream a little dream of me. Dream of me looking
into your eyes and whispering I love you as you
touch my soul. Dream of a love deeper
than any ever told.

Dream of you being loved and treated right. I'll bet it's
me who's at the source of that light. Dream a little dream
of me. Dream of rolling around in spring's fresh grass.

Dream of butterflies landing down
and kissing your finger tips
while I nibble on your lips. Dream a little dream of me.
Dream of spring time, beautiful flowers, evening showers
as my body towers yours.
As we intertwine I'd be so inclined
to make you smile over and over again, driving you
securely insane.

I'd love you totally and completely freely.
You couldn't refrain from giving me your all
as I give you all of me spiritual, mental, and emotionally
Dream a little dream of me.

Where there is bona fide love you'll find that you will be able to see God and all the splendor of His creations in all aspects of that love.

I'M LOOKING AT YOU

I'm looking at you,
I'm looking at you and I
see galaxies being formed.
When I look at you, I see
"Earths". I see "Earths"
revolving around their
"suns,"

I see purple "moons" and
high, dry, secure land in
the midst of a monsoon.
When I see you, I see me!

I'm looking at you and I
see nations springing up! I
see the strength that built
the pyramids,
I see the beauty that made
honorable pharaohs call
upon wars for the reasons
they did!

I see how earthly bodies
interact with heavenly
beings. I see the reality
that will make film
producers want to put
the beauty of your
essence on the silver
screen.

I'm looking at you and
as I see me, your
mental transcends your
physical, we intertwine,
your mind elevates
mine and I...I'm looking!

I'm looking at you and I
see the strength of ten
Zulu warriors! I look at
you and I hear the cry
of a soulful nation
thumping, thumping on
drums of umoja.

Signaling a new
beginning, and its
calming.

I'm looking at you and I
feel at one with the
universe as U-N-I-verse,
I'm looking at you and
I'm feeling serene.

I see you; I see strength,
I see you; I see purpose,
I see you; I see peace.
I'm just looking at you.

The great dispute: Is there someone for every one? Does the fact that women outnumber men disprove this theory? Is it abnormal to be with one person for life? Do we establish these bonds, these relationships once we get here on earth or were they established before we were even created? How does lasting love work, where does destiny in love relationships begin.

GENESIS

I've seen you before. Maybe in another lifetime,
on another planet, time and space. I've seen you.
While God almighty was creating me,
He was creating you too.
See, as the great Creator was creating my
right arm your left was
done.

He placed us side by side and right then we felt as one!
He formed my head, my ears, nose
and toes then He spoke
my eyes into existence. He placed a
fire burning in your belly
so hot and strong it made me sweat, and I ....
I wanted to kiss
you even though my mouth wasn't
formed yet.

God gave you a back strong enough
to carry a nation and me the
heart warm enough to nurture it.
He gave you hands to build and heal
and me the strength and the ability to assist
and reveal his real purpose.

He gave you feet lead by righteousness,
knees strong enough to bend
and be humble and legs well enough to
rise up and carry out His purpose
and I saw that. I saw you.

JOURNEY THE SOUL OF A POET

Mouths formed, lips tender and sweet...
we kissed.
I've seen you before.
You are what my soul was made for.

I've heard some say that your soul travels while you are
asleep and brings back memories from its tour.
So when you awake and you encounter
people and places that seem familiar it is because
your soul arrived at this place long before you did.
Your flesh encounter was established in the beginning....

IN THE BEGINNING

Four-thousand years before Christ scaled this earth I knew who you were and I recognized your worth.

After then when I finally came into existence your presence was near me. At night as we slept separate our souls rose, traveled and intertwined, and even then you took care of me.

As I grew my conscious beheld images of you, skin smooth like black silk, eyes deep with every gaze reaching down into the depths of my soul pulling up every emotion inside of me.

Now here you come to compliment my maternal strength, when most brothers couldn't even conceive of going the length.

I remember conversing with my cousin about my "power." He said that my match would intimidate me. I reassured him that my match would only enhance my might, feed my every need and receive every nourishment that is me. Who knew we were talking about you?

Just to see you perform is a triple pleasure. My heart mesmerized, my mind, like wise

and my body absorbs your vibrations, giving heart pounding elation not to mention emotional ejaculations. Hmmm........Listen, I don't even smoke but as the person sitting next to me drags on a Newport, I have to ask her to pass me one.
        Total satisfaction....

During the healing process it is best to get to know yourself. You must focus mainly on you. This requires you to delay certain sexual intimacies. Interaction is good but proceed slowly. Start in the mind and leave the physical behind until it is sincerely time. Only a king will be able to relate, appreciate and enjoy...

JOURNEY THE SOUL OF A POET

KING

The first time I saw you I wanted to run my fingers
through your locs. That was my first thought.
Next I envisioned myself shampooing your dreaded glory
and massaging your temples while listening to portions
of your life story.

I want to have you resting on my breast as I caress
you to sleep then stop.
I want to rub your neck then kiss your chest then stop.
Will you let me tell you a
long story by way of a whisper and brief gentle kisses
upon your ears then stop.
I mean I want to be as intimate
as we can be without breaching physical boundaries.

Now I know certain intimacies I will have to earn and
along the way I intend to learn what makes you laugh,
what makes you cry, what it is going to take to keep you
high.

I want to be the one in charge of the upkeep and the
twisting of your hair. From the peak of your head to the
soul of your feet, every inch of you I want to keep.
Then stop.

I'm not looking for a superman, I'm just looking for a good man, a real man. A man who is not afraid of a woman with her own ideas, her own money and the ability to do most things with or without a man. However, she understands the importance of having and respecting that strong man at her side.

KRYPTONITE

Most times I feel like my intellect is
kryptonite to some brothers,
We have one conversation and it's a while
before we have another.
I get remarks like "man you just be going off!"
or "you heavy, we need to finish
this." Then he gets placed on my "he need
not call back list."

How does it feel to have a man of steel
who is able to receive, process,
regurgitate and expound on topics our bond
was found. A man who can
listen, engage, and respond faster than a
speeding bullet, leap dialogue in
single bound.

Pull it out of me when I don't want to
share and understand it's not
that I don't care but I need to know that
when I do share the insides of me
mental, spiritual, emotional and physically he
will still be what I need him to
be and not what he thought I wanted him to be...

Looking back at the relationships I have had, verses the acquaintances I have made each situation met us at different places in our lives spiritually.

These days I am more prayerful, much more of a worshiper, not ashamed of it and no longer timid about it. I think a lot more. I am strong willed and I am a accustomed to doing things on my own. This brings about the question to any man that might pursue... Can you handle it?

CAN YOU HANDLE IT?

Can you handle me in the moments of my
being bound in spiritual rapture?
I mean, when I am deep into another realm
and I am moved to tears for no
apparent reason. Can you handle it?

Can you still see my sanity, my strength?
Can you give me room enough to cry out
from my soul while holding me and covering me in
prayer or standing beside me
and joining me in praise and worship?
Can you handle it?

Can you see me naked, I mean open, exposed, uncovered,
vulnerable, weak,
and afraid but still see my intensity,
my might, and my depth can you build me up still?
Can you comfort me with a silent
whisper or a single touch of encouragement with wise
strong man's guidance? Can you?

Do you even follow where I am trying to go?
Can you put your feet down solid, hard
to the floor? Can you accept and
receive my passion as a woman, mother,
wife, nurturer,
co-creator and giver of life? Can you?

Will you see my power as a dominant threat to your
manhood or a complementing

element of what makes us connect? Can you embrace me at my worst? Can you see into me first before declaring war where only love wants to be? Can you?

Can you handle it?

The hearts and minds of men; These days most "brothas" lack heart and do not use their minds. The hearts and minds of men have always been my query. So much beauty, strength, intellect, and wisdom wrapped in masculinity.

Man, God's creation made to create, provide, protect, and teach. Their souls run far and deep to reach and be reached by righteousness. Life changing men, good men, pure, real, loving, and strong. God's image and my reflection.

Self explanatory...
If you cannot show me what's inside,
you need not apply.

I WANT A MAN

I am so tired of men showing me money,
and telling me they got the
best honey. They show cars, cash, and bling,
foolish boys don't know
they haven't shown me a thing.

I want a man to take the time to show me
the mountains. Midnight skies
as it blankets the earth and beautifies the
world with its stars.
I want him to take me to a waterfall,
have me close my eyes and listen
to nature's cries.

I want him to park the car, open the sun
roof and lead me to bask in the
glorious wind driven glide of an eagle
flying to win his mate. That is a
beautiful first date.

I want him to see past my hair style,
my jeans and boots; I want him
to be able to sit my shell down and cause
the soul of me to rise up.
See past my silly hang-ups and show me... me.
What I've already seen
But keep tucked away. Any given day
through pure intellect and delicate wise
Strength he can show me a new way. I want a man.

JOURNEY THE SOUL OF A POET

NEVER HAD A LOVE

Never had a love that motivated me like
you do, never had a love that
was passionate about my mental, emotional
and spiritual growth like you.
I asked for you. As I write this an
overwhelming feeling of joy and excitement
comes over me. Tears fill my eyes and in
these short days this is not the first time
you've made me cry.

I tried to remain disconnected, to say
I was successful would be a lie.
Never had a love who's so strong, yet wise in
time to be gentle. So serious
about the needs of those within his
extension and still silly too.
That thing you told me the other night, I feel it
too.

I am grateful to have gotten my wish.
A real man, a good man, God's man to
usher me into the presence of the Lord...
I never had a love.

Welcome to my daydream...

To have a relationship with your mate where you two
connect on every level is a divine experience.
Rarely do we allow it to happen,
its a tie that meet at your souls.
The one thing that will fortify that bond is
prayer. Pray together about all things,
all the time, worship together.
Battle in the heavens
side by side.
The realms you two will reach together will change
your lives and make for an extraordinary
powerhouse of ministry.

PUT TOGETHER BY GOD

This morning I had a vision... We lay asleep in our bed, the alarm rings just in time for you to rise an hour before mine. You bring me close to you, we grip hands, and you began to pray. This is how we start every day. When you felt we should, we also got the children in to pray, the whole family.

This one particular morning you sat up in the bed and said we need to get on our knees for this one. I asked, "What's wrong baby?" You said nothing's wrong, I am just high in the spirit and feel we should be on our knees. You slid out over on my side, we knelt side by side and held strong to each other's hands and you started warring in the heavens!

Then you were brought to moans and uttering I could not make out, you were weeping, I was moved. I picked up and completed the prayer with what was on my heart not knowing that I ended up speaking the very thing you were feeling. We cried together. You told me that I conveyed what you felt but couldn't get it out.

Because we battle in the heavens all the time together like a couple ordained by God is supposed to do, I was able to finish what you started in a whole other realm! **That is a helpmate on a spiritual level.**

I thank God for you, I thank God for me and I thank
God for who we can be together.
The possibilities are endless!

Philippians 4:13 We can do all things
though Christ who strengthens us

Luke 18:27 Things which are impossible
with men are possible with God

Isaiah 54:17 No weapons formed
against us shall prosper

Remember George and Weezie of the Jeffersons? They had some crazy arguments. The thing I admired about them is that no matter how hot it would get they still respected their vows and they respected one another.

They still showed each other that the love was there and they still protected one another too. No one could say or do anything to the other even if they were in the middle of an argument.

The point I am trying to make is this, once upon a time when couples had misunderstandings they cleared them up and they worked through them. Now a days at the first sign of disagreement or stress in most relationships the two begin to creep outside of their supposed sacred bond.

No major misunderstandings needed most relationships today seem to be built on lies, and lack understanding. In truth there is no love in love relationships. The highest elevation of love is understanding.

That is what love is about. We must take the time to care, know, and understand our mates. This understanding should move beyond, "how this benefits self". It should be that if you take care of him, he will take care of you and visa versa. Through that balance because of understanding all needs should be met.

I WANT TO LOVE YOU

If Billie Holiday said, "easy living is
living for you," can I love you?
I want to love you like, back when love was
pure and strong, when
men cherished women and women respected
their men, and through it
all they held on.

I want to be devoted to you like back when
folk had nothing and family
was everything. I want to love you like all we got is us
and our offspring.

I want to love you like Ashford and Simpson,
solid as a rock! Can I, can I love you?

I want to be in love with you like it's our last
chance for romance and for love…
I want to adore you like back when life was hard for
Florida and James Evens
and it was still Good Times. I want to love you like you're
George and I'm Weezie.
It was meant to be so it should be easy.

Can I love you?

I wanna love you like we met in a past life,
like the length of the Nile
and the depth of the Atlantic, no need to
panic cause I'm in it.

I want to be committed to you like it's 1863
and we just met. Upon first sight
I knew it was you and you knew it was me.

I want to love you like, like Solomon
loved Makeda, like Boaz loved his Ruth.

I want to love you with my whole spirit and in
total truth. I just want to love you.

Everyone wants something pure, a mate you can be yourself with. Someone you can look at and see the love in them looking right back at you. We all want to be as open and uninhibited as possible and not fear judgment, abandonment, or misinterpretation. I an imagine what that would feel like and pray that I recognize it when it comes to me. I think it would go something like this

JOURNEY THE SOUL OF A POET

SOUL MATE

You are my soul's every yearning.
From the moment I saw you,
yeah that time, the first time my spirit
told me you were mine.
Despite the sublime mind play of capture and pursuit
my heart was already captivated and I think you knew it.
I spend time with you and learn my heart's own desires
I listen to your expressions and you make my soul sing.
You set my lips, hips and even my finger tips on fire!
You are where my needs for affection begin and end,
you are my man, my confidant, and my
friend. So prepare to love in this space
you and I will both come to call home, and
never have to be alone.
Don't worry about trust being tainted
by illusions of lust,
cause I was given a vision of us before
I met you and lead by the spirit
to let you Be;
as I revolve around you, my spiritual male me,
see you do fulfill all my needs, cease
my greed for affection,
make me feel secure within your protection,
wisdom, and warm embrace.
Love's greatest achievement is looking at
you and seeing my own face.

While we cannot help who we love, it is so very important that we only allow ourselves to be involved in the things that we know we wouldn't mind seeing again.

No matter how rough he or she says it is at the house, if it is not rough enough for him or for her to leave then you need to step aside and let loose ends get tied.

If it is in the best interest of other little precious ones that he or she stays then it is definitely best that you let it rest. Do not make things more complicated than they have to be.

Besides if they were willing to cheat with you don't you think they will cheat without you?

HUSBAND

See I got the feel'n you was gone love me. Now please don't mistake this or take this as an air of arrogance but the energy we traded is totally relevant and clearly stated you could be mine. I want to be blind to the fact that you belong to another. May not be very good to you but still she is wife and mother.... Don't take my need to respect as a desire to reject you because if I could I would elect you my number one my man, my only one man... This thing has to end before it starts I've never experienced such irony the agony, a married man's got my heart. You seem to play the part of the man in my own dreams and it seems that only in my dreams I could have you. Awaken by the fact that you have a wife at home. Picture me spending evenings, weekends, nights, and holidays alone.

So I'll stop, I'll stop right now to keep hearts from breaking to keep lies from making a home broken. Now we could try to be fiends but there would always be this unspoken desire, a fire with in me. See, I'll long to call you baby, want to talk to you daily and maybe see you sleeping in my bed. Play in you hair, kiss your forehead to wake you. I got to beat this and keep this from cheating me out of all I deserve, so I'll place my feelings, words and my dealings on reserve until you can be mine. I need a King to walk with, one I can have on my own time; so because you have a family I got to decline. The only king I can bend for is the husband who is mine...

Our people fought and marched.
These people were attacked brutally,
and their lives violently taken from them.

We owe it to them to vote. We must!
They fought, marched and died in our honor.
Now how will we honor them?

So I Cry

And so I cry, I cry for the plight behind us I cry for the plight ahead, I cry for those that had to live through the struggles witnessing the brutality of their loved ones and those who couldn't bear it so I cry for the dead. I cried and I cried and now I write. I write for hope, I write for the grief of Africans transported from a land affectionately known as home to a "tight packing" of only 16" to lay in on a journey 6 - 8days long.

I cry and I write, I write for the spirits of those who hover over us to make us strong, I write for the "strange fruit" that swung from trees as if born freedom in culture and the desire for equality was wrong. I write, I write and I cry....

I want to write the poems that silence hungry, hurt, and broken screams
I'd write poems that speak to Obama leading us into the reality of king's dream, poems that speak to the hearts & minds of men, make folk stand up see into themselves and recall when we were Kings & Queens again.

I write, I write and I cry. I cry and I write that even those blinded about the significance in our fight will vote. Boast not that the past is the past but look to it so we can continue to move away from it, embrace the past in order to change the future. I cry and I write. I pretend to write the poems that erase hate and replace it with enlightenment. I cry, and I write. I cry for the plight behind us and the plight ahead, I cry for those

alive who will not vote which is the same as when I cry for the dead. I cry for those who have fought, they live on in spirit speak through your votes so our ancestors may hear it.
I cry...

"I aint going no 10,000 miles to help murder and kill other poor people, if I want to die I'll die right here right now fighting you. If I want to die! You my enemy not no Chinese, no Vietcong, no Japanese. You my opposer when I want freedom! You my opposer when I want justice! You my opposer when I want equality! Want me to go somewhere and fight for you. You won't even stand up for me right here in America, for my rights and my religious beliefs! You won't even stand up for me right here at home!"

Muhammad Ali

JOURNEY THE SOUL OF A POET

WE RAISE OUR FISTS

Courage, boldness, bravery, and
spirit are the attributes of a true
soldier. Battling for the rights
of those who can't fight for themselves,
battling for an incompetent commander
in chief, not to mention an immoral thief
who is too cowardice to fight himself!

Oops! I didn't come here for that. I came
to express my pride, gratitude, esteem and
to honor our very own warrior. Today we
pay homage to you and all those that fought
beside you. We raise our fists.

We raise our fists for those we miss, we shed
a tear for the unsung heroes that aint here.
We sport army fatigued bandannas, yellow ribbons,
and the colors of "Old Glory" to show we care.
We raise our fists!

We raise our fists for those who made it back
whole mind, body, and soul. Then we raise
our fists for those who just made it back.
We raise our fists.

We raise our fists for those who have to go
away again. We bow our heads, we raise our

fists, we meditate on the almighty deity who's protection surely does exist.

We raise our fists. We raise our fists not just today, but as days go by and we silently cry. Don't want to talk, prayed and prayed our voices we lift, in our hearts, we'll raise out fists!

What has happened to the story tellers of old? Why did we stop telling stories? Perhaps it is because we were not being told stories. Story telling is a much-needed tradition, it is an art that needs to be revived! Stories help our children know who they are, who they came from and how they came to be. This will help them see clearer which way they need to go.

Story telling builds bonds, bridges gaps, enlightens and uplifts. It is a gift to be a good story teller and it is also a gift to be told stories too. Talk to our future leaders, tell them how to lead, our future teachers live so they will know what to teach. Talk to our future. Give them morals, manners, give them love and life through language. Tell your children stories, write their paths so they can live your words. They will live your words, so be careful of the stories you choose

JOURNEY THE SOUL OF A POET

TELL YOUR CHILDREN STORIES

Tell your children stories, not old cold ones,
but bold stories of strength,
courage and love; build them up to achieve the
greatness that is in them!

Tell your children stories! Not lies, do not disguise their
worth. Find the stories you hold inside you, give them
stories they can grow to make come true.

People, please tell your children stories!
Speak to their spirits, appeal to the hearts of
our own future storytellers.
Embrace their dreams and nurture all that is
good within them.
Recognize their value show it to them, and build!

Tell your children stories bold, strong,
courageous and of love.
They are great and you should tell them.
Then listen...

Every chance I get to sit and listen to an older member of my community I do so. I mean the elders who have seen things and don't mind sharing what they've experienced. It is so rear to find well-minded, healthy, positive elders in this day and time. When you think of it many of the grandparents were "grand" far too soon and are growing up with their children and their grandchildren too.

No proper cultivation, no encouragement and no wise guidance. We seem to cultivate our boys to become rappers, and encourage them to disrespect women. Girls are cheered on every time they shake to they shake to the latest top 10. I wish we could have that old time leadership again without the jim-crow pain. It seems that when we had little and endured much, we valued more. We instilled more and we took more time and pride in the family. The elders of this day are far from what they use to be.

Every chance I get to sit and listen I will....

Cherish and honor the elderly.

WISDOM'S PEARLS

I get great joy from
looking square in the eyes
deep and filled with miles
of vision.

Wrinkled skin, rich and beautiful, hair
white, hands strong and bent
from age and years of fashioning
and shaping the lives of others.

Thank God for the elderly fathers
and mothers who abide by the book
of Titus second chapter. It is at their feet
I'd gladly take a seat. Mouth closed,
ears, heart and mind open affixed in the
direction of wisdom's every breath.

For her pearls are priceless and I live
to string them upon my soul.

Wisdom, the
fruit that will make you whole.

Sugar Dish

My grandmother kept a sugar dish on
her dining table. This ghetto ass
nigga couldn't figure why I had one on mine too.
He said I was trying to
get as far from the ghetto as I possibly could
when all I was doing was
repeating what I remember was good.

He wanted me to hold on to the ghetto life,
said my values were too close
to white when my values came from a
woman whose life style would put
these ghettos to shame. No cultured bastard,
so damn lame!

I'm talking about a woman who's
mother was a slave. She had seen more
tragedy than these so called "gansta" records
ever played. I refuse to
perpetuate an admiration for the ghetto life.
I admire the elders who fought
for and taught more about a better life.

I am talking about men and women who
were driven not lead. Not even
while being shackled, whipped, hung, beaten,
castrated, decapitated
and left for dead. I have great affection
for those that create direction,
who do what is right even when it aint
popular right now.

Dance to your own music
create your own rhythm
and definitely follow your own path.
Peace

My parents must be the world's greatest!
They are highly supportive, loving, each in their own
way. I thank God for placing me with them.
I know that children are a gift, however I believe
that good parents are a gift as well and I thank God
for mine.

JOURNEY THE SOUL OF A POET

GOD'S GIFTS TO ME

From day one you've been there for me, teaching me right from wrong. Letting me know when to let go and when to hold on.

Time after time I could tell you when I've done wrong knowing that your love and understanding is so strong. I have always been able to put trust in my mom and dad.

The thought of either of you being disrespected, hurt, or sad, saddens me. I ask the Lord to keep you each night before I sleep. The very thought of losing you makes me weep.

Words cannot express my gratitude for all
you've done and continue to do. None other than the almighty God can be placed above you!
I can't say it enough, Mom and Dad I love you!

F.I.R.M.

Females In Charge Regulating Money
We as ladies are coming to the table with a mind to make money. Most times it's in male dominating fields and we still have to deal with the failed attempts of the old glass ceiling affect.

But women, we always find a way over, around and even through the obstacles we face. We set the tone, doesn't matter who sets the paste. James Brown said it best, "It's a man's world but it wouldn't be nothing without a woman or a girl."

THE F.I.R.M.

Females in this 'man" world make it mobetta. We came to get our feta. Always known as the backbone, that strong component which holds it all together.

Birds of a feather may flock together but aint no birds over here, stay clear and beware. Intelligent, independent, sweet tasting behinds, these ladies are just too profound for some uniformed minds. These ladies exude class and are still down to earth, have you any clue of a FIRM woman's worth?

Naa, of course you don't and most will never fathom these psychological spasms we deliver, make your body rock and your soul shiver, brothers come correct offer up much respect. Hold down the set with royalty as we trade loyalty and check what prosperity brings. The FIRM baby, coming down with only Queen things.

I have got to give thanks. First and foremost to God for He blessed me with the talent to tell stories and paint pictures through words. I am grateful to have been given this talent and I hope to be able to be a blessing to others by sharing and encouraging. I would also like to give thanks to the poets before me. I only hope to be as motivating and uplifting as those I marvel at.

THANK YOU!

Thank you mother sister Souljah you were before me, encouraged and molded me, showed your soul to me. Taught me that "being both feminine and strong represents no conflict," and ignorance is devoured through my own "360 degrees of power," thank you!

Mother Maya Angelou, oh where do legend poets go? Mother Maya with fire, inspired and scolded as she told it like it is. Oh mother so wise, God's blessings fall upon you as you remind a nation to rise. "Just like moons and like sons with the certainty of tides, just like hopes springing high still I rise!"

Thanks to the sisters before me and the brothers too. I'd be remised if not to mention, and wouldn't dare leave out Langston and his crystal stair.

To hear this brother's words, makes me shiver. I hope my soul too, will grow deep like the rivers. No. I pray, "oh Father forgive me for waiting till now to say how grateful I am to God for gifting me the ability close to those of legendary poets like Robert Frost, Sonia Sanchez, Paul Laurence Dunbar, and particularly Nikki Giovanni.

To hear her Ego trip puts a smile on my face as she explains with confident grace " I designed the a pyramid so tough that a star that only glows every one hundred years falls into the center giving perfect and divine light, I am bad!" I mean after listening to sister Nikki, I feel like "I... can fly... like a bird in the sky.

CONTACT PAGE
Journee Publications
P.O. BOX 901
Morrow, GA 30260

To book for speaking engagements, readings or to purchase books and cds.
Send requests to:

journeepublications.com

journeepublications@yahoo.com

For updates and more poetry go to
myspace.com/mayatheyoungqueen

www.ingramcontent.com/pod-product-compliance
Lightning Source LLC
Chambersburg PA
CBHW070642300426
44111CB00013B/2214